How Your World Really Works

Declan Flood

How Your World Really Works
Copyright © 2024 by Declan Flood
All Rights Reserved

No part of this publication may be reproduced, distributed, or transmitted in any form or by any means, including photocopying, recording, or other electronic or mechanical methods, without the prior written permission of the publisher, except in the case of brief quotations embodied in critical reviews and certain other non-commercial uses permitted by copyright law.

First edition 2024

This book is dedicated to my family, my friends, and anyone interested in finding out how their world really works.

Acknowledgments

To all my teachers and mentors along the way who are too numerous to mention by name.

You know who you are.

Contents

Preface ix

Introduction xi

Chapter 1: The World..1

Chapter 2: Focus..6

Chapter 3: God 9

Chapter 4: Jesus 20

Chapter 5: The Holy Spirit 29

Chapter 6: Fear 32

Chapter 7: Salvation 35

Chapter 8: Sacrifice...37

Chapter 9: Heaven...40

Chapter 10: Hell 43

Chapter 11: Ego...45

Chapter 12: Scarcity and Abundance 47

Chapter 13: Forgiveness.......................................49

Chapter 14: Judgement 54
Chapter 15: Possessions 57
Chapter 16: Sin 61
Chapter 17: Defencelessness 65
Chapter 18: Sickness 68
Chapter 19: Healing 70
Chapter 20: Our Father 73
Chapter 21: Cast the First Stone 78
Chapter 22: Separation 80
Chapter 23: Connection 83
Chapter 24: The Mind 85
Chapter 25: Prayer 87
Chapter 26: Religion 89
Chapter 27: Gratitude 92
Chapter 28: Happiness 94
Chapter 29: Life 97
Chapter 30: Death 99
Chapter 31: Love 102
Chapter 32: Truth 104
Afterword 106
About the Author 109

Preface

Some people wonder about the distorted map of the world on the cover. This is what the map of the world really looks like in two dimensions. The traditional map below that you are used to seeing is, in fact, the distorted version!

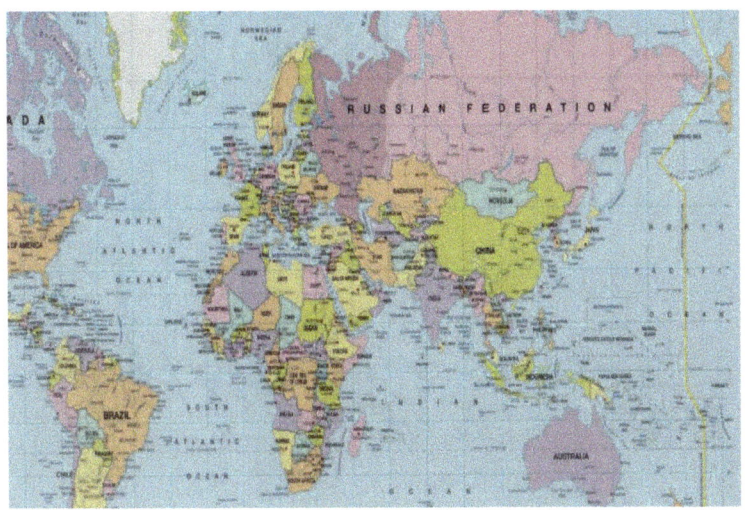

Do you know that the Equator runs through the centre of the earth? It is at the centre of the map on the cover but almost at the bottom of the map above, which is one cause of the distortion, making Europe, Russia, and North America look bigger and Africa and South America much smaller.

You can also check out the area of Australia and the area of Greenland. Greenland is 2.166 million km^2 and Australia is 7.692 million km^2. So, Australia is just over three and a half times bigger than Greenland. (3.561 times to be exact.) Now, look at the map above and see if that is the case. On that map, Greenland looks bigger than Australia! When you look at the map on the cover, it is much more accurate.

So, why is this important?

It is important because the traditional information that you have taken for granted may not be based on fact. It is based on perception, and your perceptions are shaped by your parents, relations, teachers, friends, religion, environment, government, state of mind, personality, and so many other things. This book sets out to look at some traditional beliefs and present to you a different picture.

There are a number of ideas that are repeated many times in different contexts. This is designed to help you to focus on the important concepts and to see them in a different light.

There are at least 32 other important areas where you may not have received the correct information, and the purpose of this little book is to give you a different perspective on each of them, which I hope will bring you closer to understanding how the world really works.

Introduction

Before you embark on reading the material in this book, I hope that some background information will be useful for you in deciding whether you should invest your valuable time in it or not.

To introduce myself, my name is Declan Flood. I am from a small town called Dalkey, in south county Dublin in Ireland. I have been an avid reader of all books on self-development, spirituality, religion, and motivation in an attempt to make sense of it all. I have always asked big questions like: what is beyond the end of the universe? What was there before the beginning of time? Why are we here? Is religion important? Is there a God? Do we simply die, or are we eternal?

I was brought up a Catholic by Catholic parents and went to a Catholic school. I was always drawn to the question around God and spirituality, and while I practised diligently, there were always so many things that just didn't make sense to me, which prompted the lifelong quest for knowledge and understanding. I am a natural sceptic and will question everything, which was not a trait that was appreciated by the Catholic priests and Christian Brothers back in the 1960s and 1970s.

A few years ago, a friend and fellow seeker recommended a book called "A Course in Miracles" (ACIM). I ordered it, received it, and made countless attempts to read it; I must admit, as clever as I thought I was, I simply didn't understand it. I read page after page, very slowly, and still had no idea what it was all about. The daunting prospect of 1,249 pages of very small print in three sections overwhelmed me. The language was difficult to the point of being almost inaccessible, so it sat on my bookshelf for years. I read all the chapters carefully, yet at the end, I had no idea what it was all about.

Then I found a book on Audible – "Jesus - My Autobiography". The work was channelled by Tina Louise Spalding, and even being a bit sceptical about the whole concept of channelling, I decided it was worth a listen. I was glad I did. Suddenly, it all made sense to me; the stories and clarifications were interesting, and even though it could be considered controversial, I wasn't surprised by anything and, on some level, was aware of the story even before I heard it. There were several mentions of the book "A Course in Miracles"(ACIM), and this prompted a revisit. This was made easier with the discovery that Tina recorded 365 lessons of the workbook that includes a daily commentary channelled from "the One you know as Jesus", which can be found on YouTube.

These lessons have become my start-of-day ritual, and the depth of knowledge and understanding has been truly life-changing. My day job is in education and training, and one of the things I like to do is to turn complexity into simplicity through understanding.

What I love about these lessons is that they are completely positive and life-affirming. There are absolutely no negatives. The teachings cover areas like: love, forgiveness, defencelessness, compassion, non-judgement, innocence, creativity, personal power, and using your mind to its fullest capacity. While the knowledge is coming from "The One you know as Jesus", the lessons are so good, they will work for you on a personal level, even if you are a confirmed atheist. If your own current image of Jesus prevents you from accepting this aspect of the teachings, that will be fine, so long as you approach it with an open mind, secure in the knowledge, you will not be coerced into believing anything. Maybe understanding your beliefs and where they came from will enable you to attain a higher level of personal freedom and true happiness, like you never thought was possible.

What I think has happened is that so many people have had a negative experience with religion and those who call themselves religious that they have included God, Jesus, and the Holy Spirit into the same category, and as a result, have dismissed the whole idea of spirituality or anything beyond the human or physical realm.

I am aware that when it comes to words like God, Jesus, and the Holy Spirit, most people have a clear picture in their minds as to what they think they are. These pictures are not always positive and not always accurate. The picture was embedded in your mind by outside forces, and to many people, they conjure up a very negative image. So, allow me to present a different picture for you.

God is the word for "all that is". God is the creator and all of creation. God is energy, God is light, and God is love.

Jesus took on **physical** form around two thousand years ago and is now a spiritual being who is still around and available to help you, to make sense of your life and your world.

The Holy Spirit is that little quiet and unwavering voice in your mind that is connected to all that is, separate from the ego, that guides you to peace, love, and happiness.

For each of these words, feel free to substitute any other word that you are more comfortable with. The words are not important, the message is.

You exist on two different levels — on a physical level and through your consciousness, in what is termed the body and the spirit or body and mind if you prefer. By turning everything upside down, changing your thought processes from being a physical body that occasionally has spiritual experiences to recognising you are a spiritual being, currently having a physical experience, could be the key to unlocking a new level of understanding.

What I hope to achieve is to take some of the powerful concepts contained in "A Course of Miracles" and make them more accessible to a wider audience. I will be citing other sources of information, including the Bible and some personal experiences, to clarify some of the points raised, hoping that I will maintain the essence of the message to make it simple rather than simplistic.

It is important to know that what you are reading in this book is my current understanding and interpretation of what I think "A Course in Miracles" is saying about how the world really works. It is not presented as a definitive guide, and I am sure that in many areas, I am likely to change my own opinions as my knowledge and understanding increase. I have no doubt that some academics and ACIM purists will be appalled, still, if it helps even a small number of people to find their own truth and brings you to a clearer understanding of how things really work or, more importantly, how you can make them work for you to live a happier and more peaceful life, then the exercise will be worth all the effort.

The good news is that I am not asking you to believe anything; I am not on a mission to convert the world. I am not asking you to change your religion or to join some group of free spirits chanting mantras on a hilltop. Of course, you are free to do all these things if you find them enjoyable.

My intention in writing this short and simple book is to provide you with a different view of the world, a different way to look at things and a different way to live and think. I will be sharing my interpretations of some well-known lessons and stories that have the potential to improve every aspect of your life. The big questions at the outset are: Are you ready? And will you let it?

I do not claim to be an expert or a guru or better than anyone else. I am simply the person who has taken the time to ask some big questions, went on a journey to find the answers, and now wants to share my findings with a wider audience.

It is an invitation to "change your mind" and to get you to realise that your thoughts may be far more powerful than you think, and perhaps you are not alone and in conflict with the world, even if it appears to be that way a lot of the time.

I have always wondered that maybe we have been looking at things in the wrong way, and the chapters that follow contain the explanation that makes the most sense to me.

Many people who teach about God and Jesus seem to have a need for your money. I can assure you that I am not looking to get any money from you (apart from the price of the book!). Nor am I attempting to set up a new religion. The last thing the world needs is another religion!

This book is about establishing your own personal and individual connection to "all that is" and gaining confidence in knowing that you already know what is right for you. As soon as you understand the two levels your mind works on, everything will become clear.

The ultimate purpose of this little book is for you to have a better, happier, more abundant, and peaceful life, full of all the good things that are available to you that you may be missing. So, happy reading and learning.

Best wishes,

Declan Flood

THE TRUTH WILL SET YOU FREE

Chapter 1

The World

There is no such thing as "the world". There is no single version of what the material world is. With over eight billion people on the planet, there are more than eight billion versions of reality.

So rather than thinking about "the world", you should only focus on "your world"- the world of your own creation. You create it through the decisions you make and the world you experience is the world you have created by the decisions you have made up to now.

You decide where you live. You decide who you live with.

You decide what you do for a living.

You decide to go to work or not and whether or not you work when you get there.

You decide what social media, blogs, or news channels you follow. You decide what you focus on.

It should not be surprising to you that the world you live in is exactly as you have created it.

You might say "I didn't decide to suffer abuse". The uncomfortable fact is that you did! You decided it, you live with it, you stay in it. As a son of God, you have the power to be, do or have anything you decide to focus on; that is the free will you were given, and if you want a different life, all you have to do is make a decision and stop blaming others, blaming the government, blaming the system, blaming God or anyone else for the situation you find yourself in.

The situation you are in is the effect of all the decisions you have made up to now and the only way to change it is by making different decisions.

One of my passions is gardening, and a thought that has often struck me is that everything that is in my garden is there either because I put it there or I left it there. The same thinking applies to your life. Everything you have in your life right now is because you have either put it there or you have left it there.

Every second of every day, you still get to choose what to keep and what to let go.

To understand the world, you should be aware that there are two worlds: the invisible world and the visible world. The visible world is the world of denser atoms and is seen by most as the real world. Everything that is made of atoms has a lifespan that will eventually change to a different configuration. The invisible world is the world of spirit, love, compassion, energy, forgiveness, and joy; this is the eternal world.

It is amazing that people often dismiss the invisible in favour of the material, and some think the material world is the real world. Scientists agree that the universe is made up of three different components. While the percentages vary, the best estimates are that is about 70% dark energy, 25% dark matter, and 5% normal matter, e.g., atoms. If you know anything about atoms, you will know they are about 99.9999% empty space, and rather than being solid stuff, they are simply energy at their core, vibrating energy, so in overall terms, stuff makes up a tiny part of the universe that we live in.

The world is your world; you create your own reality, and you can create it any way you want. Most people think that the "real world" is the world of physical reality, the world of stuff. The invisible world is imaginary. What if it was the other way around? What if reality is mind, consciousness, thought, dreams, inner guidance, connection, love, forgiveness, and gratitude? What if the world of assembled atoms is just the illusion you have created with your mind?

You get a glimpse of this in your pursuit of happiness. Physical objects like cars, boats, houses, and jewellery, no matter how expensive, can amuse you for a short period. The things you truly value are the invisible things like love, friendship, connection, peace of mind, forgiveness, and gratitude.

The world is like watching a movie and the projector is your mind. Trying to fix things physically is like going to the screen to bring about change in the content.

The world is simply 8 billion overlapping screens with 8 billion projectors that all are part of the one God and you get to create your own movie.

The physical world is the sum of all our thoughts and beliefs and in the realm of cause and effect. The world is the effect, and your thoughts are the cause.

The world that you observe is not something that is happening to you; it is coming from you.

I now think there are three types of people in the world:

1. There are people who look to control other people.
2. There are people who allow themselves to be controlled.
3. There are the AICM students who neither want to control nor be controlled and live their lives with courage, confidence, love, joy, and passion in full and uninterrupted freedom. Truly enjoying the experiences of physical form while maintaining contact with the non-physical. They look at everything as perfect right now and experience the pure joy of simply being.

Have you ever noticed that there are some people who bring out the best in you, and there are others who bring out your worst side? So even a materially constant being such as yourself is, in fact, a different person to the different people you interact with that also changes based on time, situations, and circumstances.

Lesson 190 is very clear: "The world you see does nothing. It has no effects at all. It merely represents your thoughts. And it will change entirely as soon as you elect to change your mind".

Chapter 2:

Focus

I have always been a firm believer in the notion that "You get what you focus on". In fact, I have added to it: "You get what you focus on ***100% of the time.***

Your life right now is a result of what you have focused on up to now. You are a co-creator with God, and even in your seeming separation through physical manifestation, you still retain the power of creation, and you get to create your own life.

Every minute of every day, you get to choose what you focus on. Do you focus on love, or do you focus on fear? Do you focus on the miracles that are happening all around you, or are you focusing on the news and the terrible things that are happening in some other part of the world?

Are you focusing on the positives, or are you always looking for the negatives? Whatever reality you focus on is the reality you will get.

Jesus said: "I have come so you would have life and have it in abundance", and he has shown us the way. The problem is his message has been hijacked and twisted.

Too many people have lumped religion, the church, God, Jesus, the Holy Spirit, and the clergy into the same category. I hope by reading this book, you will see that all are different, separate and still part of the unified whole with a special place in the complete picture.

The power of focus works on every level and all of the time. Your greatest challenge is to make sure you are focusing your mind on the right things. You have to be very careful when using the power of focus, and here are a few

pointers that I hope will help you to use this powerful tool for your own benefit.

You get what you focus on 100% of the time.

If you focus on what you want — you will get what you want.

If you focus on what you **don't** want — you will get what you **don't** want! If you focus on the wanting, then you will simply get more wanting.

You need to keep yourself alert at all times because there are so many distractions.

If you focus on Love, you will get Love. If you focus on fear, you will get fear.

If you focus on all the terrible things that are happening in the world, that is reality you will create for yourself.

If you worry, you are focusing on the things you don't want to happen.

If someone's behaviour upsets you, that is an indicator that you are focusing on their behaviour that you judge as being bad.

Rather than focusing on controlling every one of your thoughts, the easiest way to monitor your success is by focusing on your feelings. If you feel good, that is an indication you are focusing on good things. If you feel bad that is an indication you are focusing on bad things. It is that simple.

By being aware of how you feel and what you are feeling and then taking time to question all the feelings that come up, this will put you in a stronger position than simply being like a matchstick in the ocean being tossed around by the waves, with no control over your journey or eventual destination.

Chapter 3

God

Most people have a clear picture of who God is and what God does, that has been instilled into your mind from birth. You may have inherited your beliefs from your parents, who inherited them from theirs. The reality is that if you have any picture at all, by definition, it is wrong because we can only picture material things, and God is non-physical.

Whether you realise it or not, chances are that your picture of God is something like He is depicted in Michelangelo's painting of the Sistine Chapel (above). One of an old, grey-haired, white man with a grey beard and a booming voice who sits on a cloud and judges and condemns people. A God who is separate from each of us, who is capable of real-world magic and likely to take a whim and strike people down with all sorts of disasters. When people tell you that they don't believe in God, what I think they are really saying is that they don't believe in this image of God —and maybe they are right!

It is also interesting to note that in the picture above, the red shape that God is depicted within can be seen as a perfect representation of a human brain, complete with frontal lobe, temporal lobe, and medulla oblongata, which is missed by most people, maybe Michelangelo knew more than his contemporaries and had a great sense of humour.

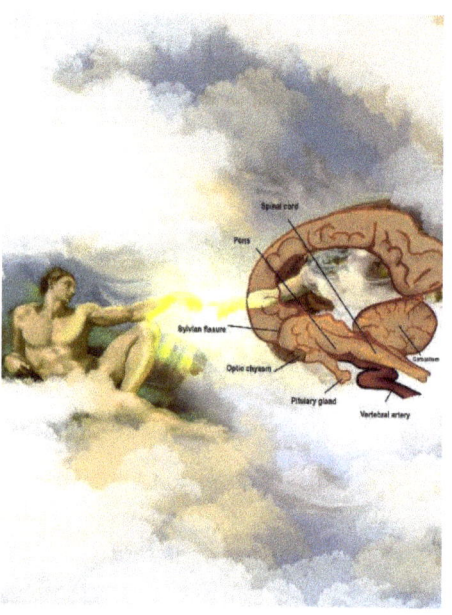

Even the most religious people see God as external to them. "God is our father in heaven", they tell you. In other words, God is there, and you are here. The English translation of the Lord's Prayer also portrays this image in the words "Our Father, who art in heaven", which suggests God is in a place called heaven, and you are here in a place called earth, separate from Him.

It also suggests that God is a person, an entity in His own right that is separate from and better than all of us.

In the Bible and in most religious texts, God is referred to as "Him". Of course, being everything as well as everywhere, God is as much female as male. In this book, to maintain consistency, I will use the pronoun "Him", it is important for you to know from the outset that this does not imply any gender bias; it is just simpler than saying he, she, and it in every sentence, and will make the book easier for you to read.

I remember from my early childhood question 6 in the Little Green Catechism that we were taught at school that asked the question "Where is God?" and the simple answer was: "God is everywhere." After many years of reading, researching, and studying, I think this could be as good an explanation as you can get.

What if, God **is** simply the word for everything and everywhere?

What if God **is** the word for the unity of the universe, the creator, the creation, and the created?

What if God is love and the light that brought everything into being? What if God is energy?

What if God exists on the level of thought? What if, God is?

And what if you are an integral part of all that is

and one in God and with God?

And not just all the people in the world, all life, all matter, all energy, all dark matter, all dark energy and all thoughts and dreams are all just different manifestations of the one God. What if we are all one? There is one line in the Bible when God said to Moses: "I am that I am" (Exodus 3:14). This might make more sense if you added a comma: "I am that, I am" where God is telling us He is everything. God is simply the "I am".

Some religious people refer to God as "The man above" — when you see God in human form and external to yourself, you could be missing the point completely. There is a saying about God looking down on us, another concept of God being "up in Heaven" and us mere mortals "down on earth". The fact that He is looking also suggests He has eyes, which also projects a physical form on what is not physical.

When you have to believe in something, by definition, doubt is implied. The Bible states very clearly, "Be still and **know** that I am God." (Psalms 46:10)

If God created you, you were created as you are, with all your talents, all your weaknesses, and all your imperfections. You are as God created you, and you are perfect in every way. The only obstacle to this is your own thinking, your own vision of what you think perfection should be and in comparing yourself to others. If you work on the basis that God is love and God loves everyone and everything, it is a far more pleasant thought, that maybe is much closer to the truth.

"I am as God created me" Lesson 94 from A Course in Miracles.

I find it easier to understand the concept of God to think in terms of a universal presence and not as a person. If God is everything and everywhere, then you are part of the same God that I am and every animal, tree, plant, and atom, as well as the consciousness, the energy, and the thoughts behind them.

It is said that God created us in His image and likeness. What seems to have happened over the years is that we have created God in our image and likeness and projected all our worst attributes on this mythical figure we call God. Over the years, God has been a human creation in myriad forms, from the Roman and Greek gods to the current religions, who are simply people telling other people what to do and how to behave and by imposing a sense of authority that this is what "God wants" — they get a much more compliant and obedient type of follower.

We have further humanised God with concepts like "The hand of God", "The face of God", "The heart of God", "The footprints of God", and when you retain these images, you are in danger of missing the whole point of God.

What if God is not a being, an entity, or a person? What if God is energy, light, or love, or simply God is?

There are passages in the Bible warning us about idols. When you try to put physical form on anything that is not physical, it completely distorts your thinking and understanding, and these images become the idols you have been warned about.

The Earth is about 150 million kilometres (93 million miles) from the sun. In terms of millions of kilometres, the whole Earth is about the same distance from the sun every day. That does not mean that everyone on Earth is experiencing a sunny day. There are clouds, there is rain, there is snow, and even smog that blocks out the sun in certain areas at certain times. There are shelters and there are umbrellas. This does not mean that the sun is shining less brightly. The sun is always there and always shining. Similarly, with God, God is always there in light and love, and when you see yourself as separate from God and each other, you are creating the clouds that prevent you from experiencing God in His fullness. Grace is the acceptance of God's love.

To take the first step to connect with God, simply look upon God as pure energy, pure light, and pure love, everything there is and an integral part of what and who you are. God is communicating with you constantly. For the message to be received, all you have to do is listen. Prayer is when you are talking to God, and meditation is when you are listening. Remember the words in the Bible: "Be still and **know** that I am God". (Psalm 46:10)

There are many passages where we are referred to as "Sons of God" — I think this was framed in an attempt to explain your link with Him. The reality is that you are even more than a Son of God; you are a part of God, and He is in you as you are in Him. We are all one in God.

God may not be communicating with you in words. He communicates with you through your thoughts, your feelings, your passions, the things you love, the things that take your breath away, and the things that make time stand still.

God is love and only love. Whoever successfully convinced the world that God is something or someone you should fear, and that God seeks vengeance, that God will judge and condemn all the sinners and will raise up the righteous, has done the world one of the greatest disservices of all time. This is a fundamental lie you must confront to get closer to the truth.

God cannot judge or condemn — God is only love.

God does not forgive because there is nothing to forgive.

God is not some external force that causes things to happen; you can do that all by yourself. Everything you have in your life right now is a result of everything you alone have focused on up to now, and that will never change.

Consider the possibility that maybe you are an eternal spiritual being who has the power to take on human form for a limited time, with a view to experience the experiences and to learn lessons. In human form, you have absolute free will and that includes either living as a part of God or in separation from Him. All fear and pain come from your own feelings of separation, and all happiness and joy come from your connection with all that is. Every minute of every day you get to choose.

In our world, we tend to see everything in a dualistic manner. There is good and there is bad, there is hot and there is cold, there is light and there is darkness, there is the creator and there is the created, and these are all separate from each other.

What if you could change your thinking and get your mind around the concept of unity or oneness? WB Yeats once asked, "How can we tell the dancer from the dance?" Most of us are stuck with the concept of duality. When you think of things as good or bad, black or white, up or down, light and dark, hot or cold, or whatever, everything you perceive has an equal and opposite.

The reality is different:

There is no such thing as darkness; there is only the absence of light. There is no such thing as cold; there is only the absence of heat.

There is nothing that is either good or bad; everything simply is. The creator and the created are one.

In the spiritual world, everything simply is.

When you think about God as your creator, you tend to think of this in your own terms, like when you make something yourself. There is the maker and there is the object, and both are separate from each other. With this thinking, you see God as separate from creation. The shift you need is to see God and creation and what is created as one. Simply "God is". So rather than seeing God as something separate from yourself, understand that God is each and every one of us and everything is all part of the one God, including you.

One of the consequences of recognising this oneness is brilliantly portrayed in Lesson 181 of A Course In Miracles: "I trust my brothers, who are one with me". Here, you are encouraged to look for the best in everyone and everything.

My abiding mantra has always been that "You get what you focus on 100% of the time." If you focus on fear, you get fear. If you focus on suspicion, you get suspicion. If you focus on a world that is out to get you, you will also get the results that come from that level of focus.

Leaving aside all thoughts of religion, of God or anything else, just by following these simple rules, you have the power to transform your life. Tim Minchin wrote the words in his song — "Not Perfect": "The weirdest thing is that this house has locks to keep the baddies out, but they're mostly used to lock ourselves in". The more you think about the truth in that line, it shows how you are constantly living in a state of fear and in self-defence to protect what you consider as your personal property when, in reality, you are simply creating a prison for yourself.

If you could suspend your fear, if you could look on everything with love, if you could truly recognise that we are all one, there is no "them" and "us", there is only "us", and in your world there is only you and the reality you perceive is the reality you create within your own mind. The good people and the bad people that you observe are simply down to your own judgement of them, and in every case, you lack the complete picture. There is a great line: "Don't judge me for the choices I have made, when you don't know the options, I had to choose from". If you can incorporate this type of thinking into your life, it will make you happier and at peace, and in this state, you are closer to experiencing the oneness of God.

Imagine a very clever fish in the ocean which is capable of thought and communication at a higher level than you imagine any fish could have. Now, imagine this wise fish talking to all his friends about what he has observed in the ocean over the past few years. He could try to convince them that in the world, there are only other fish, plants, crustaceans, some water mammals, lots of plastic, and occasionally some very large nets that suddenly appear that are better off avoided, and that is all there is.

He would rubbish the crazy notion of the concept of water. Of course, there is no such thing as water, he would say. If there was, wouldn't you all see it? No, there is no water, only other fish, plants, crustaceans, some water mammals, lots of plastic, and occasionally some very large nets that suddenly appear that are better off avoided.

As crazy as this story is, it is a better representation of the presence of God in your life because God is everywhere and everything, and like the fish, you have no other reference point. God is love, God is light, God is compassion, God is consciousness. Just as the water is indifferent to the thinking of the fish, God is also indifferent to all the thoughts that you are having and the actions that you undertake.

Of course, it doesn't help when you have religious teachers who have indoctrinated you with pictures of a bloodthirsty, vengeful God who is apart from you and is constantly punishing you for all the sins you have committed. Who sits in constant judgement and has the power to condemn you to eternal damnation should you fail to follow the path that is set out for you by the leaders of the particular church you were born into or that you decided to join at some stage in your life.

Some people spend their lives trying to find God. You will never find God by looking outside yourself. All you have to do is look inside yourself, be still and experience the connection with "All that is". Remember: "Be still and **know** that I am God".

One question often posed by people who claim to be atheists when discussing the existence of God is: "How could a God do this or do that"? The reality is that if you suspend your indoctrination for a moment and consider the information that is presented here, God does not "do" anything. God simply is. On a physical level, everything that happens to you is created by yourself. When you multiply that by the eight billion creators on the planet, the world we currently have is the only possible outcome.

Chapter 4

Jesus

This picture is the image most people have of Jesus. Even the symbol of Christianity is the cross, which results in thinking of suffering and death. When you think about Jesus, it is easier to look at three different aspects of Him. The first is the man Jesus, who walked on this planet around two thousand years ago. The second is the non-physical essence or consciousness of Jesus, who is immortal and still in constant contact with many people on the planet. The third is the image of Jesus that is portrayed by the

Churches and different groups who claim to be Christians.

The physical life of Jesus was about teaching lessons of love, forgiveness, and freedom. It was about the resurrection, not the crucifixion. His teachings are all about love. When asked what the greatest commandment is, he replied, "Love one another" or "Love your neighbour as yourself". There are different versions in different passages of the Bible. Here are a few:

Matthew 22:34-40

"Teacher, which is the great commandment in the Law?"

37 And he said to him, "You shall love the Lord your God with all your heart and with all your soul and with all your mind.

38 This is the great and first commandment.

39 And a second is like it: You shall love your neighbour as yourself.

40 On these two commandments depend all the Law and the Prophets".

Mark 12

29 "The most important one," answered Jesus, "is this: 'Hear, O Israel: The Lord our God, the Lord is one.

30 Love the Lord your God with all your heart and with all your soul and with all your mind and with all your strength.

31 The second is this: 'Love your neighbour as

yourself. There is no commandment greater than these".

32 "Well said, teacher," the man replied. "You are right in saying that God is one and there is no other but him.

33 To love him with all your heart, with all your understanding and with all your strength, and to love your neighbour as yourself is more important than all burnt offerings and sacrifices".

There is a part of this simple commandment that often goes unnoticed. When He explained how you should love your neighbour, He said: "Love your neighbour **as yourself**". So many people miss this point: You have to love yourself first.

If you fail to love yourself, you are incapable of loving anyone or anything else. In this world, most people are their own worst enemies. They criticise themselves; they abuse themselves. If anyone else on the planet spoke to you the way you speak to yourself, would they be your friend? Would you like to spend more time with them? Probably not. This is the first thing you have to put right for everything to work as it should.

When Jesus was asked why He came, he answered clearly: "I came so that you would have life and have it in abundance" or "I came that they may have life and have it abundantly". Depending on what version of the Bible you are reading. In all versions, the overall message is clear: His mission is to show us all how to live a better life. Unfortunately, over the years, His message has been twisted, misunderstood, and manipulated by different groups and religions in pursuit of their own agendas. Now is the time to put this right.

You see people who claim to be Christians shouting about morality, sin, damnation, gender, sexual orientation, about what they claim are "Christian values", and nothing could be further from the truth. If they understood the first thing about the teachings of Jesus, they would know that His only commandment is to love one another, and that means everyone and everything.

I could not find it recorded that Jesus ever claimed to be *The* Son of God. He always referred to himself as "The son of man". Even at the end, when Pilate asked Him, "Are you the son of God"? He replied, "It is you who say that I am". (Mark 15:2) As The Son of Man, he took human form and spoke with human words to help everyone to see through the illusions and to live glorious and abundant lives.

He did say, "I and the Father are One" (John 10.30). From the earlier section on God, you should now see how this claim could be true. We are all "Sons of God" as part of creation. Jesus, too, was a son of God, albeit with a deeper connection and greater understanding than most people who have ever lived, and He came to show us the way.

He referred many times to God being his father, and from this, He was known as The Son of God.

The purpose of Jesus' life was not the Crucifixion. It was the Resurrection that showed us all the way to eternal life. Be clear: eternal life is not something that will happen in the future; eternal life, by definition, is now and always. He showed us there is more to us than our physical bodies, and we all have eternal life, whether we realise it or not.

While not with us physically, Jesus is still with us in non-physical form, still looking to make a connection with you and to show you a better way. The book "A Course in Miracles" (ACIM) is a new form of contact to clarify His teachings on a wide range of topics. The material was received by Helen Schucman in the 1960s and 1970s, and the source of the teachings identified Himself as Jesus. As you read through the pages, the Workbook, and the Manual for Teachers, it becomes clear that this is no ordinary course, and the material is far above anything anyone else has ever written.

A Course in Miracles tells us that we are all sons of God. "As the Son of God, you are the light of the world" (Lesson 61)

When you read the teachings of Jesus in the Bible, there are two main things you have to keep in mind: firstly, He was talking to the people of that place and time in a language they could understand, and secondly, he spoke in Aramaic, which is a much more complex language that either Greek or English that the Bible has been translated into. With different translations and different agendas, some of the messages became distorted over time, and the Course in Miracles sets out to correct the distortions by bringing clarity and wisdom that you are most welcome to participate in.

Jesus was (and is) a rebel. He would not conform to the powers that be in his time on our planet, and now in spiritual form, is no different. He is constantly communicating with all who are open to listening to Him and there are people who are tuned into His frequency and are worth a listen. You can make up your own mind about the validity and the power of the messages based on your own instincts.

From all my readings the simple message Jesus brings is one of absolute freedom. Freedom from all the things you do to hold yourself back. Freedom from the programs you have running in your head, freedom from fear, freedom from judgement, freedom from worry, freedom to live your life to the fullest. He truly loves you and only wants the best for you. If you can look past the twisted images that you have been indoctrinated with, look past the lies and the deceit, past the people who spread fear and suffering in His name. to the true message, everything makes sense, and everything is only wonderful.

Jesus urges you to follow your passions, to do the things you love doing and to do them your own way. You are how God created you, and you are perfect in every way; you are a perfect version of yourself. All you have to do is get past your own idea of being separate from God, past your limiting beliefs, look past everything you perceive as negative and realise that the only way anything is negative is because you have chosen to perceive it as negative. It is your world, and you can create it any way you want it to be.

Rather than running on automatic pilot all day long, constantly reacting in a defensive way, constantly judging people and situations, all you have to do is stop and realise that this moment is absolutely perfect and what is happening right now is a result of everything that has happened up to now and the present moment couldn't possibly be any other way.

The good news is that things can change, things can improve, things can get better and for that to happen, all you have to do is change your point of focus or change your mind. Focus on the positives, not the negatives; focus on love, not on fear; focus on forgiveness, not on revenge; focus on abundance, not on lack; focus on happiness and making others happy; focus on what is real and not on illusions; focus on the invisible and not the physical, and you will bring about such an amazing change in every aspect of your life, that you will become unrecognisable over time.

Jesus said, "Peace I leave with you; my peace I give you". (John 14.27) Some people may wonder how that has worked out for Him over the years! The answer is that it worked out perfectly! As with any gift, there are two parts: giving and receiving. Peace is given to you, and you can choose to either accept it or you can choose to ignore it.

The way to live in peace is to forgive everything and suspend your judgement of everything. Easier said than done! Still, it is worth the discipline, and if peace is important to you and you value a quiet mind, then it is worth consideration and action.

When Jesus said, "The poor you will always have with you" Mark 14:7, John 12:8, Matthew 26:11. I have always thought that this was spoken with sadness and regret rather than a grim prediction for the future or permission for any group of people to keep another subdued. The poor are those who fail to learn the true message that Jesus came to deliver and fail to see their own worth and value. They live lives of poverty and fear, irrespective of how much or little money they have in the bank. You can focus on abundance; you can focus on lack, and either way, you will get what you focus on 100% of the time.

Jesus has been given a bad image over the years by fanatical religious people who have completely misunderstood His message and what he came to do. So many of his teachings have been edited out of the Bible, and the ones that remain have been twisted to enable controlling empires to be built. A Course in Miracles is all about putting the records straight; it has come at this time because, particularly in the West, people are freer now than at any point in history. You can read whatever you want, you have freedom of speech, and you can believe whatever you choose to believe without fear of being thrown in jail or burned at the stake!

My motivation in writing this book is to give you a fresh look at these topics and hope you will find the concepts presented making more sense to you than a lot of the explanations you have received up to now. By seeing how this is solely for your own benefit and how it is in no way manipulative or controlling. You are not required to sign up for anything; you are not expected to believe anything; you are not required to stop, start, or continue anything.

You simply apply the relevant lessons to your own circumstances and enjoy the benefits.

At the time Jesus lived on the planet in physical form, the Romans and the Jews seldom agreed on anything. They both agreed that Jesus would have to be put to death, as His teachings of personal freedom were too radical and dangerous and had the potential to upset the status quo.

In the years that followed, some of His teachings were destroyed, and others were kept and twisted to suit the agenda of the people who were either editing the script or translating it into different languages. The result of all these teachings is so far removed from what Jesus intended. A Course in Miracles was offered as a way to return to the truth and it is that truth this book invites you to explore.

Chapter 5

The Holy Spirit

The picture most people have of the Holy Spirit is of a white and radiant dove. Which, of course, is another one of these idols that you were warned about.

The Holy Spirit is the bridge between your illusory perception of the world and the truth of your divine nature. The Holy Spirit is the voice of truth and love within you that can help you to see beyond your illusions and recognise the unity of all things.

The Holy Spirit is the source of guidance and inspiration that can help you navigate the challenges and difficulties of life. The Holy Spirit is always available to you, and you can learn to listen to its voice through a process of inner listening and prayer.

The Holy Spirit is not a separate entity from you; it is the truth of your own being. It is the part of you that is connected to God and all of creation, and it is always present within you, even when you are not aware of it.

The Holy Spirit is also the source of healing and forgiveness. Through the power of the Holy Spirit, you can release all your illusions and negative beliefs and experience a profound sense of peace and love. The Holy Spirit helps you to recognise your true nature as a divine being and to see the world and others through the eyes of love and compassion.

The duality you experience in your mind is explained as the ego mind that promotes your separation from God and The Holy Spirit that connects you to the mind of God.

For the atheists among you, who struggle with the notion of The Holy Spirit, can call it any name you like. You can call it "unity consciousness", "your higher mind", "your intuition", or even the process of being "in the flow".

What matters is your recognition that you are more than just a collection of atoms that came into being at birth (or conception) and will die and go into the ground to decompose. You and your body are not the same thing. You say "I have a body". You wouldn't say "I am a body" because, at some level, you know you are more than just a body. You have thoughts, dreams, emotions, and feelings that cannot be explained purely as a physical state.

I have heard people rubbish the notion of God and Spirit, and when talking about life, they say something like "I believe it is just all atoms". My question is: where are the atoms in thoughts? In consciousness? In joy? In inspiration? In music? In writing songs or poetry? In love? In emotions? In forgiveness? In non-judgement? In peace of mind?

Anyone who has had the sad experience of being at the death bed of a loved one will know that the second before they passed and the second afterwards, the exact same atoms are present on the bed, still everything has changed forever. There has to be more to life than simply atoms.

By connecting with the part of yourself that is beyond atoms, by letting go of all notions of separation, you will feel the difference, no matter what you call it.

Chapter 6

Fear

On the very first page of the introduction to the text "A Course in Miracles", it clearly states that the opposite of love is fear. In later lessons it explains that every action you take is either guided by love or fear. Or, to put it a different way: every action is either an expression of love or a call for love.

The message Jesus brought was for all of us to choose love.

It is also clear that fear and worry mainly apply to material things and anything that you perceive to be a personal possession.

Fear is the root cause of all your negative thoughts, emotions, and behaviours. Fear is a product of your ego, your false sense of self that you create when you identify with your separate body and the world of form.

Fear is not real but is a projection of your own beliefs and perceptions. When you believe in the reality of fear, you create a self-fulfilling prophecy that reinforces your sense of separation from God and everyone else.

The antidote to fear is love, and it is the only thing that can truly heal your mind and bring you back into alignment with your true nature as a divine being. Through your practice of forgiveness, you can learn to let go of all your fears and negative beliefs and experience a profound sense of peace and joy.

You can also learn to recognise and release your fears through a process of inner listening and prayer. By turning to the Holy Spirit, the voice of truth and love within you, you can learn to see beyond your illusions and recognise the unity of all things.

By recognising the illusory nature of fear and turning to love, you can learn to release your fears and experience a profound sense of peace and joy in your life.

If all this talk of God, Jesus, and The Holy Spirit is getting a bit much for you, you can still substitute any of the words with any other words you like. Even ignoring the spiritual aspects, moving away from fear is a good idea for you to work on to improve the quality of your current physical existence, even if you want to avoid what you might perceive as the woo-woo world!

If you live in fear, if you focus on fear, all you can get is more fear and more things to be feared. By changing your mind, by changing what you look at and how you look at it, you will change everything.

With the arrival of 24-hour news channels, you are treated to non-stop fear-mongering. You are shown all the worst things that have happened in the world over the past day or days, according to the particular news provider you choose to allow to fill your head. There are threats from criminals, murderers, terrorists, the next virus to spread across the world, governments, the corporate world, the health of our ecosystem, to the demise of our planet. All these are presented to you on a daily basis just to keep you in a state of fear.

If all these frightening images are not enough for you, you can also use your leisure time to go to the cinema or turn on the movie channel on your TV and watch the latest horror movie that is guaranteed to scare the life out of you.

Please be aware, you are choosing what news channels you watch, how long you watch them for, and you choose what movies you see! By filling your head with fear, you are lowering your own vibrational levels, and you are making yourself miserable. Always remember: "I could see peace instead of this". (Lesson 34 AICM)

Chapter 7

Salvation

You don't have to die to achieve salvation; it can be done in the comfort of your own mind, and you can fully experience it right here on earth while alive in your current body, and you can do it right now. You don't have to believe in God to achieve salvation, you don't have to believe in Jesus or the Holy Spirit, and you don't have to follow a particular religion. You only have to believe in and desire salvation.

Salvation is about being saved from torment, pain, lack, poverty, and what you perceive as evil, and to achieve it, all you have to do is change your mind.

There is no judgemental God out there to get you; there is no hell where you will suffer eternal punishment. Salvation is a choice you make, and you can make it right now before you turn the next page.

The only thing you need to be saved from is yourself. It is your own mind that has the power to punish you far worse than anybody or anything else. Your mind is a collection of beliefs you have picked up either consciously or unconsciously from other people, other organisations, or other teachings that you have chosen to accept.

Even at this early stage, I hope you are beginning to see that the only problem here is you, and the good news is that the only solution is also you.

Chapter 8

Sacrifice

Sacrifice is pointless. It is a human limitation placed on humans by humans. In God's world of abundance, there is absolutely no need for it, and a God who is everything and is everywhere would have absolutely no need for mere mortals to kill things to make Him happy.

Sacrifice is a central concept in the ego's thought system, which is based on the belief in separation and lack. The ego believes that to gain something, you must first give up something else and that sacrifice is necessary in order to achieve your goals.

Sacrifice is not necessary for spiritual growth; in fact, the belief in sacrifice is a major obstacle to your awakening. True spiritual growth comes not through sacrifice but through the recognition of your inherent oneness with God and all of creation.

The idea of sacrifice is rooted in the belief that you are separate from God and each other and that you must strive to earn God's love and approval through your actions and deeds. However, this belief is an illusion. You are already one with God and with all of creation. You never have to earn God's love and approval; you have it always. You are the way God created you, and His love is always available; you only have to tap into it.

Instead of sacrifice, the Course emphasises the importance of forgiveness and the recognition of your shared identity as a divine being. Through forgiveness, you can release your attachment to the ego's thought system of sacrifice and embrace the truth of your inherent oneness with God and all of creation.

The concept of sacrifice is central to many of the religious rituals and practices of the Israelites and early Christians. Sacrifice is seen as a way to atone for sin and to gain God's favour or forgiveness.

In the Old Testament, there are many instances of animal sacrifices being offered as a way to seek forgiveness or to thank God for the blessings received. In the New Testament, the sacrifice of Jesus on the cross is seen as the ultimate sacrifice, through which

God offers salvation and forgiveness to all who believe in him. In reality, Jesus went through the crucifixion process to demonstrate to all that there is life after death. Even though our bodies die, our consciousness lives on forever. You can call it consciousness, spirit, soul, or whatever you like.

If you believed for one minute that we are eternal conscious beings, then the fate of one body in one lifetime in one moment in time does not constitute a monumental sacrifice by God or Jesus or anyone else.

Laying the guilt on every individual for the suffering and death of Jesus by telling them that Jesus died for their sins is the method used to maintain followers for the types of religions that promote this kind of thinking. No sacrifice was made, there are no sins that need to be forgiven and no further sacrifice is required.

It is reported that when on the cross, Jesus said the words, "Father, forgive them for they know not what they do". (Luke 23:34)

Chapter 9

Heaven

Heaven is being in a state of bliss, and you don't have to die to attain it. Heaven is all around you all the time; you only have to access it.

Heaven is not a physical place but a state of mind or consciousness. It is the experience of perfect love, peace, and unity with God and all of creation.

Heaven is not something that you earn or achieve through good deeds or religious practices, but rather, it is your natural state of being that you can access by releasing your attachment to the ego's thought system of separation and fear.

In the Bible, heaven is often depicted as a physical place, a realm where God resides and where believers will go after death. It is often described as a place of eternal joy and peace, where there is no pain or suffering, where you are reunited with loved ones, and where there is eternal happiness and bliss.

While there are some differences in the way heaven is depicted in A Course in Miracles, the Bible, and common perception, there are also some similarities. Both the Course and the Bible emphasise the importance of releasing attachment to the ego's thought system and cultivating a state of love and peace in order to access heaven.

There are also some differences in the way heaven is perceived in different spiritual traditions. The common thread is a state of ultimate peace, joy, and unity with God (All that is) and all of creation.

As long as you maintain notions like "The Pearly Gates" and the personification of God as a resident in a place called "Heaven", you are heading down the wrong path. Heaven is available to you as a state of consciousness at all times, you only have to focus on accessing it and eliminating your own personal judgements on the events that are unfolding around you.

You can access heaven right now, you can access peace, joy and tranquillity simply by changing your mind.

Chapter 10

Hell

In the Bible, Hell is often described as a physical place of punishment, a realm of existence where sinners are condemned to suffer eternal torment and separation from God. It is often associated with the concepts of judgement and punishment, with those who have lived a sinful life being condemned to Hell.

Hell is often described as a state of separation from God. On that basis, most of the world's population is living in hell right now.

Hell is mainly associated with religious beliefs and is seen as a place where the soul experiences eternal suffering and punishment.

Hell could not be a physical place of punishment. It is a state of mind in which you experience fear, guilt, shame, and separation from God and others that you can transcend through forgiveness and the recognition of your shared identity as a divine being. It is a state of consciousness in which you feel cut off from the love and peace of God and experience suffering and pain.

Hell is a great selling point for most of the major religions, who have convinced people that without their intervention (in return for your personal and financial support), this is how you are going to spend the rest of eternity.

With this fear so firmly engrained in most people, even the most die-hard atheists sometimes use religion as an insurance policy, just in case the teachings are real.

Chapter 11

Ego

A Course in Miracles defines ego as that part of you that you recognise as separate from God. It is a false sense of self, which is the root of all your fears, conflicts, and suffering. The ego is the voice of separation, which leads you to believe that you are separate from God and others. It creates the illusion of individuality and personal identity. The ego is the source of all your negative thoughts and emotions, such as fear, anger, guilt, and anxiety, and is the primary obstacle to your experience of peace, love, and joy.

Your ego is not your true identity; it is a false self that you have constructed out of your beliefs, perceptions, and experiences. You can overcome it by shifting your identification from the ego to your true self, the spirit, the divine, or the consciousness within you. This involves letting go of your attachment to the ego's illusions and recognizing your shared identity with all of creation.

The ego is not something to be fought against or eliminated but rather something to be recognized and released through the process of forgiveness. By forgiving yourself and others, you release its hold on your mind and open yourself up to the experience of realizing your true identity as a divine being who is powerful beyond measure.

The ego is focused on the body and the material world. Your mind and your consciousness are eternal parts of you and go on even after the body has outlived its usefulness.

Chapter 12

Scarcity and Abundance

Most people are familiar with the concept of scarcity and abundance. They are present in both the Bible and A Course in Miracles, but their interpretations differ slightly.

In the Bible, scarcity is often associated with lack, poverty, and want. For example, Philippians 4:19 says, "And my God will supply every need of yours according to his riches in glory in Christ Jesus". This suggests that God provides for us and meets our needs, even in times of scarcity.

Abundance, on the other hand, is often associated with prosperity, wealth, and blessings. Deuteronomy 28:12 says, "The Lord will open to you his good treasury, the heavens, to give the rain to your land in its season and to bless all the work of your hands". This suggests that God blesses you with abundance when you follow His will. Or at least what the religious leaders tell you what His will is, which we have seen already, may or may not be based on truth.

In A Course in Miracles, scarcity is viewed as a state of mind that is based on fear, lack, and limitation. It teaches us that scarcity is an illusion and that abundance is your natural state. You can experience abundance by shifting your perception from fear to love and by recognizing that you are connected to the infinite source of all abundance.

Abundance, according to the course, is not just about material wealth but also about experiencing peace, joy, and love. You can experience abundance by focusing on your spiritual growth and cultivating a sense of gratitude and generosity.

Chapter 13

Forgiveness

Forgiveness is everything. You must forgive everyone for everything they have ever done, and most importantly, you must forgive yourself. That might sound like a daunting task, but maybe by explaining it differently, it will become more achievable for you.

When you hold a grudge or seek revenge, the only person you are hurting is yourself. The Buddha said: "Holding on to anger is like grasping a hot coal with the intent of throwing it at someone else. You are the only one who is getting burned". The longer you hold on to it, the more damage it will do to you and to you alone. The person for whom it is intended has no idea and cares less that you are torturing yourself.

If peace of mind is important to you, then forgiveness is the force that will bring it to you. When you listen to some of the leading motivational people and spiritual teachers in the world, people like the Dali Lama, Eckart Tolle, Deepak Chopra, Oprah Winfrey, and the like, you will notice that there is great emphasis on the power of forgiveness and not surprisingly it is sometimes explained as a selfish act as the person who will benefit most from your forgiveness is yourself.

Forgiveness is the means by which you release yourself from the pain of your past experiences and open yourself to love and peace. Forgiveness is not about excusing the behaviour of others or denying the supposed harm that has been done to you; it is about recognizing that your perceptions are limited and that you can choose to see things differently.

The ego is the source of all conflict and pain in the world, and forgiveness is the way to undo the ego's hold. By forgiving yourself and others, you release yourself from the ego's cycle of attack and defence and open yourself to the guidance of the Holy Spirit, which will lead you to a state of true peace and joy.

In the New Testament, Jesus teaches that forgiveness is essential to our connection with God and that you must forgive others if you want to be forgiven yourself. In the Lord's Prayer, Jesus teaches us to pray, "Forgive us our trespasses, as we forgive those who trespass against us" (Matthew 6:12). This emphasizes the importance of forgiveness as a two-way street and tells you that you cannot expect to receive forgiveness if you are unwilling to forgive others.

The Bible also teaches that forgiveness is a choice you must make, and that it is not always easy. In Colossians 3:13, you are told to "bear with each other and forgive one another if any of you has a grievance against someone. Forgive as the Lord forgave you". This verse reminds us that forgiveness is not just a matter of saying the words but of truly letting go of your anger and resentment and choosing to love and forgive others as God loves and forgives you.

You need to understand that as you go through your day, the only thing you are experiencing is your own consciousness. Yes, it seems to be other people, places and things that are causing your troubles. The reality is that all your troubles are the creation of your own mind. Everything is neutral until you pass judgement on them. Then, it is your own judgement that causes all your pain.

So, if you want to lead a happy, peaceful life, look at all things with love. Forgive your parents; they only did what they thought was the best they could do at the time.

Forgive your siblings; anything they have done that you perceived as negative is simply them acting out of fear, not knowing what they did.

Forgive your friends, your family, your neighbours, your business associates, your governments, and everyone and everything else.

See everyone you encounter as a great teacher who has come into your life to teach you a valuable lesson. Some bring easy lessons, some bring joyful lessons, some bring hard lessons, and some bring really difficult lessons. You will keep getting the same lesson in different guises until you learn it and move on.

Forgiveness is the key to happiness. (ACIM Lesson 121)

When I hear someone on a news report following a tragedy saying words like "I will never forgive them for what they have done", I feel really sorry that they have chosen to carry this pain with them indefinitely. I truly hope that you, who are reading these words, will take this passage very seriously and look to integrate forgiveness into your everyday life. It could be the greatest gift you could ever give to yourself and everyone around you.

Everything you have ever done in your life was motivated by where you were at the time and who you were with. Everyone does the best they can with what they have got at that moment in time. Of course, there can be decisions you have made that you might like to change. Still those experiences and the lessons learned have made you the person you are today, and if you would like a different future, simply make different decisions today. There are also times when something terrible happens and you despair. Years later you look back and realise that that was the best thing that could have happened.

Without all the past events, you couldn't have this moment. This moment is perfect. So, rather than waiting years for the realisation to dawn on you, forgive everything as soon as it happens and wait in joyful expectation to see how it is going to unfold.

The most important decision you can make is to forgive everybody for everything and, most of all, forgive yourself.

As powerful as forgiveness is, there is one thing that is even more powerful: non-judgement. If you can master non-judgement, then there is no need for forgiveness because there is nothing to forgive.

Based on what you have learned so far, can you now see that God could never forgive you because there is never anything to forgive. The false teachings that we are all sinners and in need of God's mercy is the device used by religions and cults to keep you locked in because, without their involvement, you will surely be doomed to eternal damnation and burning in the fires of Hell. A loving God could not condemn or punish anyone or anything. A loving God sees us as mere children who "know not what they do".

Chapter 14

Judgement

This is one of the most misunderstood concepts that has caused so much pain throughout history. To live a truly happy life, you should stop all your judgements. The Bible is clear: "Judge not, lest ye be judged" (Matthew 7:1). To live in peace, you must switch off all your own judgements of everyone and everything.

As God is, everything else simply is. It is only your own judgement that makes some things right and other things wrong and the only person who suffers from all these judgements is yourself.

Judgement arises from the belief in separation, which leads to the perception of differences and labelling of things as good or bad. This perception of separation is an illusion, and judgement is seen as an attack on the truth of oneness. You can release judgement by recognizing that we are all interconnected and by choosing to extend love and forgiveness to yourself and others.

The Bible also talks about the negative consequences of judgement. In Matthew 7:1-2, Jesus says, "Do not judge, or you too will be judged. For in the same way, you judge others, you will be judged, and with the measure you use, it will be measured to you". This passage suggests that judgement is a two-way street, and that when you judge others, you are also inviting judgement upon yourself. The point that most people miss is that the judgement you invite upon yourself will come from yourself.

Similarly, in Romans 2:1-3, Paul warns against judging others, stating that "you, therefore, have no excuse, you who pass judgement on someone else, for at whatever point you judge another, you are condemning yourself, because you who pass judgement do the same things". Here, Paul suggests that you are capable of the same faults and failings, and that judgement serves only to divide us.

Judgement is a hindrance to spiritual growth and a barrier to love and forgiveness. Instead, you are encouraged to extend compassion, understanding, and forgiveness to yourself and others, recognizing that you are connected to everyone and everything else and that your true nature is one of love and unity.

To remain in a place of no judegment should be your main priority. As easy as it sounds, it is one of the most difficult things you can do. Simply to be and to observe.

I am sure you have had an experience in the past when something you perceived as terrible happened. For example, you lost your job or a partner left you. At the time, it seemed like the world had ended and there was no way back.

Looking back after many years, you often find yourself saying something like: "At the time, I thought it was terrible and it has turned out to be the best thing ever! If they hadn't left, I would never have met my current partner" or "If I stuck at that job, I never would have explored this new career that I really love".

This happens all the time, and if you roll back the clock, you will see that the only thing bad about the situation was your own judgement of it at the time, and once again, you have proved the notion that everything always works out for the best in the end. If you could accept that at the time of change, it would reduce so much of your needless, self-inflicted, pain and suffering.

Chapter 15

Possessions

John Lennon, in his great song "Imagine", made the statement, "Imagine, no possessions".

Seeing things as yours is the cornerstone of all worry and strife. "This is my house"; chances are the house was there before you moved into it and hopefully will be there long after you are gone, so to claim ownership is a futile exercise. You are merely the custodian of it for as long as you want to live there or as long as you can keep up the mortgage payments!

Your true identity should not be based on your possessions or external circumstances. In fact, your focus on possessions can distract you from your spiritual growth and true happiness. Possessions are part of the illusion of the physical world you need to let go of in order to experience true peace and happiness. True abundance comes from your connection with your inner self, rather than from accumulating material wealth.

The Bible cautions against being too attached to material possessions. Jesus taught that it is easier for a camel to pass through the eye of a needle than for a rich man to enter the Kingdom of God. This doesn't mean that it's impossible for wealthy people to be spiritually awakened, but rather that your focus should be on your inner development rather than just accumulating possessions that, at best, will only bring fleeting happiness. Just for your information, the Aramaic word that was translated as "camel" could also be translated as "rope".

There is an important word here and that is the word "attachment". No one is telling you not to have things or to get things. You have an amazing world full of so many toys to keep yourself amused. There are so many opportunities to make life easier and more enjoyable, and these should be welcomed and embraced. Enjoy the things without becoming attached to them and without identifying with the things, knowing that "this too shall pass". Accept their arrival and departure with joy and move on to the next adventure with joyful anticipation.

The concept of attachment can also be associated with people, such as my partner, my children, my friends, etc. The problem here is that if you identify people as "yours", you will expect them to act in a particular way. Most parents want perfect children, and what they mean by perfect is that they constantly behave in a way that is pleasing to them. We all know that this never happens and can be the cause of many arguments and stress.

Parents sometimes see their children as an extension of themselves. If their children behave in a particular way, they see that as a reflection of themselves, and that is why they get annoyed; it bursts the bubble of the illusion of perfection they feel they need to project into the world.

Expecting a partner to do and say the things that make you feel good all the time is a form of selfishness that just adds more stress to your life.

You should be grateful for everything everyone does for you, and if this could be combined with zero expectations, it would have such a positive impact on your life and your relationships. The concept of control comes from the ego; wanting to control other people, situations, and events can never be fully achieved and will always lead to conflict.

See your possessions merely as toys you get to play with for a limited time, complete in the knowledge that they have a lifespan. See people as individuals who are on their own path, learning their own lessons and always doing what is right for themselves.

Of course, we can offer opinions and ask questions to help that person see if their actions bring them closer to joy or conflict. Particularly with children, parents have a responsibility to help them become the best version of themselves, and not some form of mini-me, as often parents use their children to live the life they wished they had, and this will always end in tears.

Children are not your possessions; they are your gift to the world.

Chapter 16

Sin

Jesus is very clear in A Course in Miracles that there is no such thing as sin. You are mere children and, as such, incapable of sinning in the eyes of God. The sins you create are in your own minds. You would not scold a toddler for stumbling when they are learning to walk or attack a five-year-old if they misspelt a word phonetically. There is a famous and often misunderstood line about sin in the Bible where Jesus says, "Whoever's sins you forgive, they are forgiven them. Whoever's sins you retain, they have been retained" (John 20:23).

The Catholic Church has interpreted this as being addressed to them, where, through confession, they have the power to forgive or retain a person's sins. I think it is addressed to each of us individually, and in that context, it makes much more sense. If you forgive someone, you clear your own peace. If you seek revenge, you carry the pain with you. The only person you are damaging is yourself. The concept of sin is one of the greatest problems with our current mortal lives. If you see other people as guilty or if you see yourself as guilty, then you have been programmed to believe that punishment is deserved. If you can't find anyone willing to punish you, you are well capable of doing it to yourself!

You can easily give unconditional love to a baby. One reason is that you perceive the baby as guiltless and without sin. As the person grows up, your faculty to judge and condemn them increases. What if you could look on everyone as you would look upon a baby, as guiltless, innocent, and free from sin? Yes, people make errors, and anyone who is not currently living a life of absolute bliss is making errors right now.

In A Course in Miracles, the term "sin" is used to refer to any thought or action that is not aligned with love, which is the essence of your true nature. Sin, therefore, is not a moral or religious concept but rather a recognition that you have fallen out of alignment with your true identity as an expression of love.

The concept of sin is the result of the ego's belief in separation from God, which leads to fear and a sense of lack or limitation. This belief in separation is the root of all negative thoughts and behaviours, such as judgement, anger, and guilt.

The way to overcome sin is through forgiveness, which is the practice of releasing your judgements and grievances and recognizing the love that underlies all things. By forgiving yourself and others, you return to a state of alignment with your true nature as expressions of love, and sin loses its hold over you.

Maybe a personal story will help to explain this concept of sin. Many years ago, we had the honour of hosting two boys from Chernobyl for a few weeks. They were about 10 or 11 years old at the time. It is funny that some of the things we took for granted were a source of amazement for them, and the one thing that had them transfixed was the fruit bowl in the kitchen.

On the first evening, they went to bed, and the next morning, when they were having breakfast, we went into their room to make the beds. We discovered two apples hidden under the pillow. Our reaction was one of almost pity that they feared apples would be all gone in the morning. They obviously planned their "raid" when we were all asleep and snuck into the kitchen, grabbed the two apples, and went back to hide them in the room.

Thinking back, they were probably nervous about committing this "crime" and fearful that they would be caught, and then could have created a scary story for themselves about the consequences of their actions, which could include being removed from the house and reported to the authorities, and their Irish adventure would be over before it began. In simple terms, they could have punished themselves for their "sin".

For us, no crime was committed, and no consequence would ever be delivered.

This story is a simple analogy about us humans doing things that you are conditioned to believe are "sins" and then you punish yourself accordingly. An infinite loving God could not be capable of seeing anything you do as a sin. With infinite love comes infinite understanding. In the presence of God, there is no sin, just errors that you make that add to your learning while you are in material form.

From A Course in Miracles - Lesson 122 Forgiveness offers everything I want. "1 What could you want forgiveness cannot give? Do you want peace? Forgiveness offers it. Do you want happiness, a quiet mind, a certainty of purpose, and a sense of worth and beauty that transcends the world? Do you want care and safety, and the warmth of sure protection always? Do you want a quietness that cannot be disturbed, a gentleness that never can be hurt, a deep, abiding comfort, and a rest so perfect it can never be upset?

2 All this forgiveness offers you, and more. It sparkles on your eyes as you awake, and gives you joy with which to meet the day. It soothes your forehead while you sleep, and rests upon your eyelids so you see no dreams of fear and evil, malice and attack. And when you wake again, it offers you another day of happiness and peace. All this forgiveness offers you, and more".

Chapter 17

Defencelessness

We see the world, not as it is, but as we are.
— Anaïs Nin

You have a choice: you can look at a world full of love and kindness, with everyone doing the best they can with what they have got within the circumstances they find themselves in. Or you can look at a world full of evil, fear, threat, and danger. Whichever way you choose to look at is the world you will see.

The epitome of the later style of thinking is encapsulated within the gun culture in America. Everyone has the right to carry arms and the only way to defend yourself from someone with a gun is to have (and be prepared to use) a bigger gun. Anyone who sees a need to carry a gun is feeding into the fear culture that has the potential to lead to a downward spiral, with painful consequences for all concerned.

Jesus gives you the answer in Matthew:

{5:39} But I say unto you, that ye resist not evil: but whosoever shall smite thee on thy right cheek, turn to him the other also.

{5:40} And if any man will sue thee at the law, and take away thy coat, let him have [thy] cloke also.

If you can learn to live in complete defencelessness, you remove all fear. This concept of defencelessness applies not only to material goods but also to opinions and beliefs. You do not need to defend your own opinions; they are simply your opinions and if people have different opinions, that is their business. At no stage do you need to feel threatened or defend your chosen path. It is yours; it is the correct path for you right now. You will know if you are on the correct path by the way you feel. If you feel good, it is right. If you feel bad, it is wrong. Simple!

In my defencelessness my safety lies. – ACIM Lesson 153

The truth is that if you resort to violence even in self-defence, it is you who are attacking, and you will be the main loser, no matter how things transpire. By accepting that everything is perfect right now, that everything is exactly how it should be, should allow you simply to observe everything as it is, without the impulse to change things to your current version of what you think is right.

What you do should be right for you, and what everyone else does should be right for them. Even if they are making what appear to be grave mistakes, they must need the lesson and the learning that will come from these actions.

If you are moved to use your greater knowledge to point them to a better and easier way (as I am doing in this little book), then do it from the position of an observer and never succumb to the temptation of forcing anyone to do anything they do not want to do. You can point it out, then walk away with no attachment to the outcome; that is up to them.

They will keep repeating their own lessons until they learn them for themselves, and while you may be able to help them see things in a different way that will be beneficial to them, it is the other person who has to integrate the changes – not you! You can only change the things that are of greatest benefit to yourself.

Chapter 18

Sickness

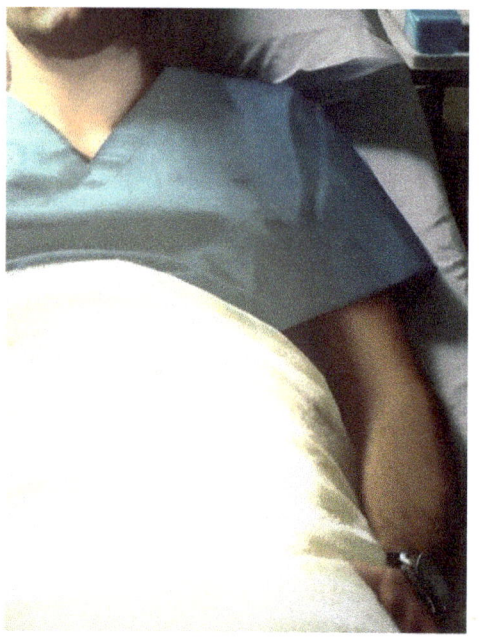

Sickness all begins in the mind. It is your way of torturing yourself, and if you can get your mind in the right place, your body will automatically follow.

Sickness is a physical manifestation of a deeper mental or spiritual disturbance. The course teaches that all illness is ultimately a reflection of a belief in separation from your true nature as a spiritual being and the corresponding guilt and fear that arises from this belief.

All sickness is ultimately a result of a mind that is not at peace. True healing involves releasing your attachment to ego-based beliefs and instead connecting with your true spiritual identity. This can be achieved through practices such as non-judgement, forgiveness, gratitude, and cultivating a deeper awareness of your true nature.

I know that when it comes to things like cancer, COVID and other conditions where we currently do not know the true cause, this lesson is difficult to accept. And even harder when it comes to sick children or babies who have not yet developed egos or a sense of separated identity. Still, as we progress, we are becoming aware that stress is a bigger factor in illness than previously thought, which is the first step to realising that the body follows the mind.

Chapter 19

Healing

Healing is the process of aligning the mind with the truth of your oneness with God or with "All that is". This involves a shift in perception from a belief in separation and fear to recognising your true nature as a conscious, spiritual being.

All physical and emotional problems are ultimately rooted in a belief in separation from God and from each other. Therefore, true healing requires addressing this underlying belief and shifting your awareness to the truth of your interconnectedness.

The mind is the cause of all experiences, and true healing comes from a shift in perception rather than from external remedies or interventions. This is because all external forms are ultimately illusions and do not address the root cause of your suffering.

The process of healing in ACIM involves the practice of forgiveness, which is the recognition that there is no separation between yourself and others. Through forgiveness, you release your belief in separation and invite the presence of love and healing into your life. Healing is a journey of awakening to the truth of your divine nature and unity with all of creation. It is a process of remembering who you truly are and returning to the awareness of your oneness with God.

Healing is not just about the physical body but about the whole person - body, mind, and spirit. It encourages you to look beyond the surface symptoms of illness and instead focus on the underlying causes, which often lie in your thoughts, beliefs, and emotions. You have the power to heal yourself by changing your thoughts and beliefs and connecting with your true spiritual nature. Through this process of inner healing and transformation, you can experience true health and well-being on all levels of your being.

One line Jesus used after healing the two blind men.

{9:29} Then touched he their eyes, saying, According to your faith be it unto you.

After he cast out a devil from a mother's daughter…

{15:28} Then Jesus answered and said unto her, O woman, great [is] thy faith: be it unto thee even as thou wilt. And her daughter was made whole from that very hour.

These are important passages for the believer and non-believer alike. Jesus did not perform magic or proclaim to be a physician! He didn't even claim to have cured the people in question; what he put the cure down to was their own faith. Their own belief was the determining factor in the cure.

We see many occurrences of people being healed from what should have been terminal illnesses. Many of these cures are put down to different things, e.g., a trip to a holy place, praying to a particular saint, having a holy relic that is said to bring healing, their own internal strength, or maybe even an incorrect diagnosis in the first place.

No matter what anyone may believe, the reality is that healing always happens within your own mind, and it doesn't matter what you believe is the cause. The fact that you fully believe is all you need to make it work, as can be seen with the placebo effect in medicine.

Chapter 20

Our Father

There are lots of people out there who will tell you that Jesus said the words "Our Father" and told us to say the words. This is not true on two levels.

1. Jesus did not speak English, so He would never have said the words "Our Father".

2. He never commanded to say the words. He gave us much more than a prayer; He gave us a template for prayer that you will see later.

The actual words he spoke were in Aramaic that were recorded as follows:

1. ܕܒܫܡܝܐĂ(ḇūn d-ḇa-šmayyā)

2. ܫܡܟne(tqaddaš šmāḵ)

3. ܡܠܟܘܬܟtê(tē malkūṯāḵ)

4. ܒܐܪܥܐ ܐܦ ܕܒܫܡܝܐ ܐܝܟܢܐ ܨܒܝܢܟ ܢܗܘܐ nehweh(ṣeweeyanakh aykanna ḏ-ḇa-šmayyā ʾāp̄ b-ʾarʿā)

5. ܝܘܡܢܐ ܕܣܘܢܩܢܢ ܠܚܡܐ ܠܢ ܗܒ ha(ḇ lan laḥmā ḏ-sūnqānan yawmānā)

6. ܠܚܝܒܝܢ ܫܒܩܢ ܚܢܢ ܕܐܦ ܐܝܟܢܐ ܚܘܒܝܢ ܠܢ ܫܒܘܩwa-(šḇoq lan ḥawbayn ʾaykannā ḏ-ʾāp̄ ḥnan šḇaqn l-ḥayyāḇayn)

7. ܒܝܫܐ ܡܢ ܦܨܢ ܐܠܐ ܠܢܣܝܘܢܐ ܬܥܠܢ ܘܠܐwlā(ṯa-alan l'nisyōnā ʾellā p̄aṣān min beesha)

8. Mitol ddeelakhee malkutha whaila. Wtishbohta la-alam almeen Amen – Because yours are the kingdom and power and the glory.

The opening words were translated into Latin as Pater Noster and then into English as Our Father.

Aramaic is a complex language where different words have different meanings depending on their context. According to Greg Braden, "Ăḇūn d-ḇa-šmayyā" literally translates as "Birth-er of the Cosmos" and neṯqaddaš šmāḵ translates as "May your name be kept Holy", which changes the meaning somewhat and it is easy to see why this translation would not sit well in a patriarchal society. According to Aramaic scholar Dr Rocco A Errico, there is another possible translation for Ăḇūn, and that is "Beloved".

The Aramaic word for forgive is shwak which also means to untie, to loosen, to set free. So, when you forgive, you set yourself free from the error that was created.

Another line that could have been mistranslated is "wlā ṭa-alan". This was translated as "Lead us not into temptation" when it could also be "Do not let us enter (or ensnared, saturated by) into temptation", which makes more sense as God would not be capable of leading us into temptation!

"Beesha" is translated as evil. There are many different meanings to this word including: bad, ugly, error, cruel, mistake, rotten, unripe, sour, immature, unfortunate, unlucky, wicked, wrong, diseased, and incorrect. As a noun, it can mean a culprit, a deceiver, a troublemaker, or someone who is bent on doing wrong.

Temptation can also be translated as materialism.

Wtishbohta is translated as glory; it can also mean all songs and praise.

la-alam is from the ages.

almeen is throughout all the ages.

Amen was used as a legal verbal contract. I will follow up, I am behind it, until it is followed up.

There is another line that many commentators miss when they proclaim that this is the prayer that Jesus told us to say. He was asked the question, "Master, how should we pray"?

Again, the exact words of His answer change depending on the version of the Bible you are reading. Here are some examples:

"In this manner therefore pray ye" (Matthew 6:9) King James Version.

"After this manner therefore pray ye" (Matthew 6:9) American Standard Version.

"Therefore, you should pray like this" (Matthew 6:9) Christian Standard Bible.

The overall message is constant, what Jesus is giving us is much more than a prayer or words of a prayer; He is sharing with us a **template** for prayer. A template that is repeated in all of the great prayers. This template has three parts:

Part 1: Recognition of the deity.

Part 2: Clear positive request for what you want.

Part 3: Give thanks.

So, in the traditional Our Father:

Our Father, Who art in heaven, Hallowed be Thy Name. Thy Kingdom come. Thy Will be done on earth as it is in Heaven. **This is the recognition.**

Give us this day our daily bread and forgive us our trespasses as we forgive those who trespass against us. And lead us not into temptation but deliver us from evil. **This is the request**.

For thine is the kingdom, The power, and the glory, For ever and ever. Amen. **This is the thanksgiving**.

In the Hail Mary:

Hail Mary, Full of Grace, The Lord is with thee. Blessed art thou among women, and blessed is the fruit of thy womb, Jesus. Holy Mary, Mother of God, **This is the recognition.**

Pray for us sinners now, and at the hour of death.

This is the request.

Glory Be to the Father, and to the Son, and to the Holy Spirit. Amen. **This is the thanksgiving**.

You can now make up your own prayers using the prescribed template Jesus gave you, and as long as the template is intact, it will be valid. Remember, "Ask and it will be given to you"? (Matthew 7:7) or "Ask, and you will receive" John (16:24) or my favorite "And whatever you ask in prayer, you will receive, if you have faith" (Matthew 21:22).

Chapter 21

Cast the First Stone

Even non-Christians are familiar with the story of the woman who was brought before Jesus having "being caught in the act of adultery" and who, under the law, should be stoned, so they asked Jesus, what should they do?

This was a very clever ploy as he was teaching his message of love and forgiveness. He could either say, "Let her go", then He would be advocating breaking the law, or He could have said, "Stone her", which would run counter to all his teachings. He said something like, "Let him who is without sin among you, cast the first stone" (John 8:7), and then from the oldest to the youngest, the crowd dispersed. Most people think that is the punchline; there is more….

After making the statement, Jesus was writing words in the sand with a stick. He looked up after a few minutes and the only person left was the woman herself. Jesus said to her, "Was there no one to condemn you"? She said, "No, Lord". Then He replied clearly, "Neither do I condemn you".

If there ever was a clear statement on the "sin" of sexual activity, this could not be clearer. These teachings are completely at odds with the so-called religious people and puritanical Christians who put such emphasis on the "sin" of sexual activity. These ideas are coming from somewhere other than Jesus.

Chapter 22

Separation

You have many examples of the idea of a twin brain and mind. The creative right brain and the logical left. "The Ego and the Id" by Freud, the human brain and the chimp brain by Steve Peters. In "A Course in Miracles", they have different names for the same phenomenon – the ego and the Holy Spirit.

The ego is the part of your mind that believes you are separate and individual, and the Holy Spirit is the universal mind that you always have access to, should you choose to explore it. In Greg Braden's book, "The Divine Matrix", he puts forward the idea of a proven connection that joins us all together.

The concept of "separation" refers to the belief that you are separate from everyone else and from God; this belief is the root of all fear, pain, and suffering in the world. Separation is an illusion; in reality, you are part of a unified consciousness or "Oneness" that is known as God. The course emphasizes the importance of recognizing this unity by practicing non-judgement, forgiveness, and love to dissolve the illusion of separation.

By letting go of the belief in separation, you can experience a state of peace and happiness that is beyond the limitations of the physical world. The process of undoing the belief in separation involves changing our perceptions and attitudes and opening ourselves to a higher spiritual understanding.

The one area that highlights separation and causes the most pain is the notion of keeping secrets. Keeping secrets creates inner conflict; trying to hide something from others is the greatest form of mental torture you can inflict upon yourself. We all know that at some point, the secret will be revealed, and at this point, the sense of relief that is experienced can be truly liberating.

When we consider separation, one way to look at it is to consider a laptop. It has two states: the first is as a stand-alone device complete with hardware, software, and files. Then consider the same laptop when it is connected to the internet. It is the same atoms and the same hardware, except now that it is connected, there is no end to the information it has access to.

It is the same for our bodies. As long as we view them as separate entities, relying on our own resources, we are limited; as soon as we acknowledge our connectedness with all that is, we move to a far higher level. To access these higher states, all you have to do is nothing! Just meditate, turn your own brain off for a few minutes and feel the difference.

Chapter 23

Connection

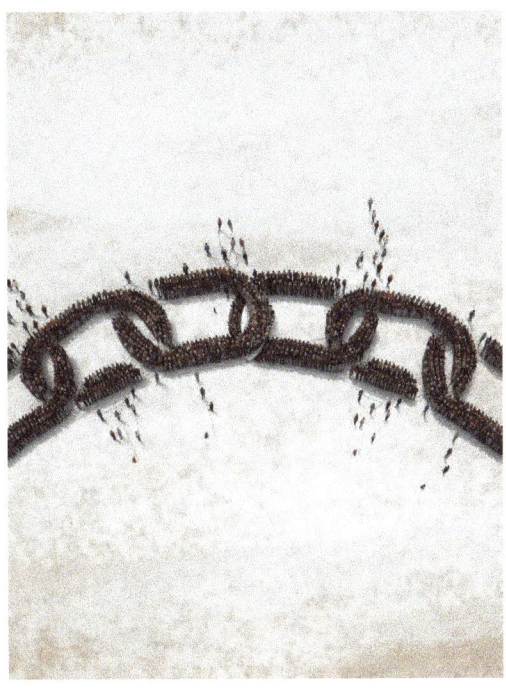

On the level of the ego, you are separate and fighting for your fair share of what is available in a world defined by scarcity. On the level of the Holy Spirit, you are one in God.

The concept of "connection" refers to the recognition that you are part of a unified consciousness, which is referred to as God or the Holy Spirit or The Divine Matrix. This recognition is the antidote to the illusion of separation and is a fundamental aspect of the course's teachings.

Your true identity is not the individual ego-self that you typically identify with but rather the shared self that you share as an expression of God. This shared identity is always present, even if you are not aware of it, and your goal should be to cultivate its awareness.

Through various practices such as forgiveness, prayer, and meditation, the course aims to help individuals experience a deeper sense of connection to others and to the divine. This connection is the key to experiencing true peace and happiness, available to everyone, regardless of beliefs or background. It is important to cultivate an awareness of this unity to experience a more fulfilling and joyful life.

Chapter 24

The Mind

There is great confusion between the brain and the mind, and many people use these terms interchangeably. The brain is the local physical apparatus while the mind is split, part is connected to the universal mind and to everyone and everything else, and the other part is the local individual mind, the ego mind, which harbours the idea of separation.

The concept of "the mind" is central to understanding the teachings of the course. It defines the mind as the source of all perception and interpretation of the world. Your mind is seen as the instrument through which you make decisions, perceive yourself and others, and ultimately experience either fear or love.

The mind can be split into two parts: the ego and the Holy Spirit. The ego is the aspect of the mind that is rooted in fear, separation, and individuality. It is the part of you that creates a sense of separation from others and from God, leading to feelings of guilt, anger, and despair.

In contrast, the Holy Spirit is the aspect of the mind that is rooted in love, unity, and connection. It is the part of you that recognises your true identity as part of a unified consciousness and helps you to connect with all others and with God.

Your experience of the world is determined by which part of the mind you identify with and listen to. When you listen to the ego, you experience fear, conflict, and separation. But when you listen to the Holy Spirit, you experience love, peace, and unity.

If living in peace is important to you, it is important to cultivate a deeper understanding of your own thoughts and perceptions and to choose to align yourself with the aspect of the mind that leads to peace, love, and acceptance.

Chapter 25

Prayer

When it comes to prayer, there are two schools of thought. On one side, there are people who believe that prayer is powerful and it works. On the other side, there are people who think it is a load of rubbish. What if they are both right?

You have seen in the section on healing that it all comes down to what you believe, so if you believe it works, it works. If you believe it is all rubbish, then it is all rubbish. There is evidence that anyone who prays with clarity and absolute belief is far more likely to have positive outcomes.

Philippians 4:6 - Do not be anxious about anything, but in everything by prayer and supplication with thanksgiving let your requests be made known to God.

Mark 11:24 - Therefore I tell you, whatever you ask in prayer, believe that you have received it, and it will be yours.

While this was written a long time ago, anyone who has read Rhonda Byrne's international best-selling book or seen the video called "The Secret" will recognise that this is the central message she summarises as "Ask, Believe and Receive".

In James 2:26, we read, "Faith without works is dead". I take this to mean that yes, having faith is important, and then you have to do something about it, take action in the direction of where you want to go, and that will make it work for you.

Chapter 26

Religion

Religions were created by people to control people. The message of Jesus has been misrepresented and distorted over the years to the point where it is now truly damaging. If you can quote God as your source, then that makes you special and gives you added authority. Add into the mix a bit of fear of eternal damnation if you fail to do exactly what they tell you to do, and you have a subservient audience.

I was born into a Catholic family, went to a Catholic school, and lived in a very Catholic country (Ireland in the 60s and 70s). I saw the Catholic Church, God, Jesus, and the Holy Spirit as one and the same. I believed that the Catholic Church was following the teachings of Jesus and worked with that concept for many years. I remember, even at a very young age, there were things that didn't make sense to me; still, I was told that to be a good person, you had to be a good Catholic, so that became my belief and as a result, I went along with it.

I could overlook the scandals, the child abuse and the questionable financial dealings. Then there came a point, sparked by A Course in Miracles, where through reading, listening, trying to understand, and living the course, I changed my mind completely.

I am not here to knock religions; I know there are some very good people, doing some excellent work, firm in their faith, which is a great source of comfort for themselves and others.

Some of what they teach is great, while some is damaging. I was inspired to write this book as my attempt to put things into perspective.

You may have seen so-called Christians carrying signs like the one above that clearly demonstrate that they have no understanding of either God or Jesus. As God is love, God is incapable of any form of hatred, and Jesus' simple message was "Love one another". I have always wanted to ask one of these sign-carrying Christians four questions:

1. Do you believe God made the world and everything in it?
2. Do you think God is stupid?
3. Do you really believe that God hates fags?
4. If He does, why does He continue to make so many of them?

Chapter 27

Gratitude

Gratitude is one of the most powerful and underutilised forces you have access to. Whether you believe in a God or not, giving thanks for everything you have is a great way to live.

Take time to look around and see all the great people and all the great things that you have. Your family (well, maybe some or most of them!), your friends, your home, your stuff, your health, your mobility (even if that is a wheelchair!), your interests, your passions, your hobbies, your body, your mind, the amazing planet we live on, the vast galaxy we live in, your food, your quiet place, your brain, and your mind, to name just a few.

There is so much to be grateful for and time should be spent to recognise and appreciate this.

There is a hidden message in the Bible about gratitude that I would like to point out to you. As well as giving thanks for what you currently have, you can also give thanks for the things you would like to happen.

There are a number of stories in the Bible, including "the loaves and the fishes", where it is recorded that Jesus gave thanks before feeding the multitude. Before he raised Lazarus from the dead, "Jesus lifted up his eyes, and said, Father, I thank thee that thou hast heard me" (John 11:41). When He was asked to have dinner with the disciples on the road to Emmaus, He gave thanks, and He also gave thanks twice at the Last supper.

What is important here is that Jesus gave thanks for the miracle before the miracle happened. By giving thanks for the miracle, the miracle had to unfold.

Chapter 28

Happiness

Happiness is the goal of all goals. Happiness is completely an internal process; other people and things will not make you happy. It is your appreciation of people and things that make you happy. Happiness is a state of mind, and you have access to it all the time if you choose to do so.

Some people think, "if I have that house, I will be happy"; "if I have a million euros, pounds, or dollars, I will be happy"; "if I have that beautiful partner, I will be happy"; "if I drive that type of car, I will be happy"; "if I own that yacht, I will be happy". All too often you look around at all the people who have all these things, and they are miserable.

As soon as they get the house, they want a bigger and better house. As soon as they get the money, they want more, never taking the time to work out how much is enough. As soon as they get a partner, particularly if their choice of partner is based on looks, they will be naturally attracted to younger and prettier potential partners. As soon as they get the yacht, they want a bigger and then bigger and then bigger still to fill a void created by the ego, which can never be satisfied.

Some people are so busy jumping from one goal to the next, they don't enjoy and appreciate what they have now. Some eternally seek things they haven't got.

Just because happiness is your natural state, it doesn't mean that it is normal! Most people torture themselves with fear and guilt that cloud their thinking and mask the happiness available to them in every moment.

The motto of the ego is: "to seek and never find". It tortures you by always keeping you one step away from everything. "If my husband stopped drinking, I would be happy". "If I had that car, I would be happy". "If I won the lottery, I would be happy". If this is your only thought process, you will find something else to be a barrier to your happiness and keep you another step away. Things will never give you happiness; it is your appreciation and enjoyment of the things that bring about happiness. Happiness is simply a thought process and a decision you can make at any time, irrespective of how much or little you have.

No matter what is happening in your life, you can always choose happiness – why not?

Chapter 29

Life

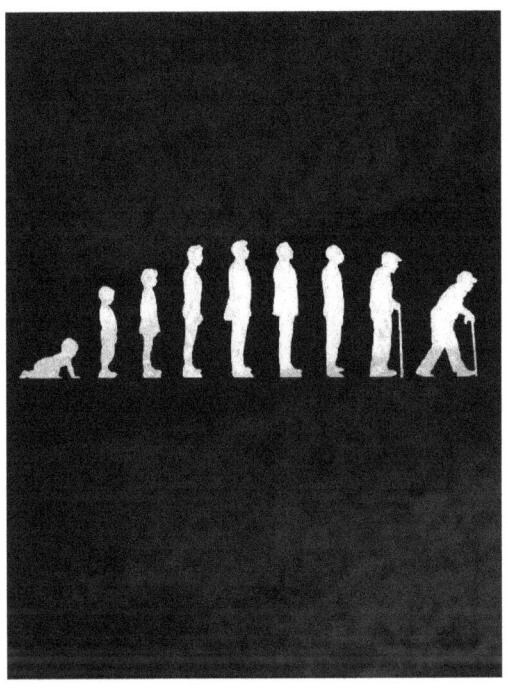

Human thinking is that life begins with birth (or maybe conception) and ends with death. On a physical level, this is correct. The reality is that you are a spiritual and eternal being who has taken on physical form for a limited time to live, learn, and experience experiences. As a spiritual being, or if you prefer the words conscious being, your body, being made of atoms, has a lifespan; your consciousness remains in non-physical form eternally.

In non-physical form, we make the decision to take on human form, and there is a school of thought that says that non-physical form is the stage where you decide your entry point to the planet and also your exit point, when the lessons you have come to learn and the experiences you have come to experience have been completed.

For your peace of mind, it is easier to look at everybody as a spiritual being who is here on their own journey and on their own path. You do not know what their mission is or what they are here to experience, hence the emphasis on non-judgement.

In life, there are two ways of looking at everything: you can see that everything is happening to you, or you can see it as happening for you or being created by you. It all depends on how you look at it. One of the big differences that ACIM teaches is the requirement to take responsibility for your own life, your circumstances, and everything that happens and to see this as a true reflection of everything that has gone before. Stop looking around you to find someone else (or God) to blame for the situation you find yourself in. You got yourself into this situation for a reason, and you are the only one who will get yourself out of it.

Chapter 30

Death

So many people are confused on this topic. On one hand, you are told you are mortal, and on the other hand, you are told you are eternal. You are told you will never die; still, you have been to funerals and know that your own death is inevitable. So, how can these two seemingly opposite positions be reconciled?

You need to go back to your true nature, which is a combination of both physicality and consciousness. Your consciousness, your mind, your spirit or your soul, whatever word you find it easiest to work with, are the eternal part of you. Your body is the mortal side of you. So, your body will die, and your consciousness will continue for eternity.

You are a spiritual being who has taken on a physical form for a limited time; you get to choose when you arrive and when you leave. You choose your circumstances based on the experiences you are looking to have or the lessons you need to learn.

All religions tell you that death is not the end, and if you truly believed that, you would no longer go around in fear of death, be it of yourself or others, and if you truly believed that, you would never grieve at funerals. We have all heard people say about loved ones who have passed that they know they are with them…. and they are.

The expression of grief you have experienced or witnessed is your own feelings of loss at the other person being taken away from you. Part of the problem goes back to the section on possessions, so on some level, you see them as yours. Your parent, your partner, your friend, or your neighbour's child. Another part is that feeling of loss combined with the knowledge that you will not see them again in this lifetime and that you will miss them being around. This is natural; you form bonds with people and the finality of knowing they are gone can be hard to cope with.

I have witnessed many times when a person's life comes to an end with the death of a partner. Sometimes, they pass away themselves in a matter of weeks and in some cases, while physically they survive for many years, they simply give up the will to live and withdraw into either solitude or alcohol or some other addiction to ease their pain.

Do you think that the person who is gone wanted to see the one they loved being miserable? It is not being disrespectful to them to go on and live out your remaining years in the best way possible.

Chapter 31

Love

When Jesus talks about love, the easiest way to make it real is to simply look at all things with love. Love is outward focused. Love is unconditional. Love is seeing the best in everything.

In Og Mandino's great book "The Greatest Salesman in the World" The Scroll marked 2 – has the following instructions:

I will greet this day with love in my heart.

And how will I do this? Henceforth will I look on all things with love and I will be born again. I will love the sun for it warms my bones; yet I will love the rain for it cleanses my spirit. I will love the light for it shows me the way; yet I will love the darkness for it shows me the stars. I will welcome happiness for it enlarges my heart; yet I will endure sadness for it opens my soul. I will acknowledge rewards for they are my due; yet I will welcome obstacles for they are my challenge.

While also written in Biblical language, these are simple and practical lines on how to put the concept of love into practice on a daily basis, without getting too immersed in soppy sentimentalism.

Chapter 32

Truth

The truth will set you free. There is only one version of the truth. Being eternal, it is indivisible.

Finding the truth involves recognising the illusions you have created in your mind and seeing beyond them to the reality of your own true nature.

You have created a world of illusions in which you believe that you are separate from everyone else and from God. This illusion is maintained by the ego, which encourages you to identify with the physical body and the material world and to pursue external goals that can never bring lasting fulfilment. The mission of the ego is to seek and never find.

To find the truth, you must first recognise the illusions you have created and be willing to let go of them. This involves a process of introspection and self-examination, in which you become aware of your own thoughts and beliefs and question whether they are based on truth or illusion, whether they are based on fear or love.

Ultimately, finding the truth in A Course in Miracles means recognising your true nature as part of the unified consciousness or "Oneness" that is God. It involves letting go of the illusions of separation and fear and aligning yourself with the aspect of the mind that is rooted in love and connection.

Afterword

I hope you found the content interesting and easy to follow. Of all the ways the world is supposed to work, which have been explained to me throughout the years, this understanding is the clearest, most consistent, and the least ambiguous I have ever found. It all makes sense and merges the knowledge of ancient wisdom, the Bible, and A Course in Miracles with life in the 21st century and provides a great working platform for all.

Even if you are as confirmed an atheist now as you were at the start, and even if you believe it all to be far-fetched; the notions of God, Jesus, The Holy Spirit, immortality, consciousness, and all that other stuff are just all made up nonsense. On a purely practical level, the application of the key learning points can still be of value to you to lead a happier, more peaceful, and fulfilling life.

Here is a list for quick reference:
1. You get what you focus on 100% of the time – So take great care to ensure you are focusing your mind on the right things. Focus on what you want and not on what you don't want. Stop focusing on the wanting and focus instead on the getting and the enjoyment it brings.
2. The only one who can hurt you is you – You can torture yourself far more with your own thoughts than anyone else can.
3. Thoughts are things – they are the starting point of everything.

4. Look at everyone and everything with love – the world will become a much better place.
5. Turn off all your judgements of everyone, everything, and every situation you find yourself in; accept the perfection of everything as it is right now.
6. Follow your passion and spend your time doing what you love with the people you love.
7. The opposite of love is fear – be aware of which one is motivating you in every moment.
8. The only thing you can fully control is your thoughts – spend as much time as you can working on this, and stop trying to control anyone or anything else.
9. There is no such thing as a neutral thought – every single one is either bringing you closer or further away from where you want to be.
10. Your feelings are your guidance system. When you feel good, you are on the right track. When you feel bad, you are on the wrong track.
11. Everything in your life is there because you either put it there or left it there. Take full responsibility for your own current situation. Based on all the things that have happened up to now, it could not be any other way.
12. Nobody else is to blame for the position you find yourself in.
13. Keep reading and learning, and place peace of mind as your greatest goal; everything else will fall into place.

14. The only meaning of life is the meaning you give it.
15. Stop comparing yourself to others; everyone is unique, different, and equal.
16. Heaven or perfect happiness can be achieved in this lifetime if you allow it to unfold.
17. The present moment is perfect in every way. Stop all thoughts of the past and the future, and enjoy the eternal now.
18. You are being constantly bombarded with illusions, always look past the illusions to the truth.

About the Author

Declan Flood is from a small town called Dalkey, in south county Dublin in Ireland. He has been an avid reader of all books on self-development, spirituality, religion, and motivation in an attempt to make sense of it all. He has always asked big questions like: what is beyond the end of the universe? What was there before the beginning of time? Why are we here? Is religion important? Is there a God? Do we simply die, or are we eternal? He has been reading "A Course in Miracles" for a number of years and presents his thoughts on the material in an attempt to make the material more accessible to a wider audience.

www.ingramcontent.com/pod-product-compliance
Lightning Source LLC
Chambersburg PA
CBHW041145110526
44590CB00027B/4132